Act Out

Thirteen Plays to Act and Develop

David Walker

Edward Arnold

© David Walker 1980

First published in Great Britain 1980 by
Edward Arnold (Publishers) Ltd
41 Bedford Square, London WC1B 3DQ

Edward Arnold (Australia) Pty Ltd
80 Waverley Road, Caulfield East
Victoria 3145, Australia

Reprinted 1981, 1983, 1984

British Library Cataloguing in Publication Data

Walker, David, b. *1947*
   Act out.
   I. Title
   822'.9'14   PN6120.A5

ISBN 0-7131-0484-8

These plays are copyright. Permission must be obtained for
all performances and recordings except when the performance
is for an exclusively school audience. Applications should be
made to Edward Arnold (Publishers) Ltd., 41 Bedford Square,
London WC1B 3DQ.

Set in 11/12pt IBM Journal by Tek-Art, Croydon, Surrey.
Printed and bound in Great Britain at The Pitman Press, Bath

Act Out is a collection of thirteen short plays specially written for 11-13 year old pupils. The plays are designed to provide a starting point for the pupil's own work as well as an enjoyable exercise in reading and performing.

Suggestions for further work are included after each play. They begin by introducing ideas for discussion and lead into activities which include library work, writing and drama.

The plays can be used in whole class groups or smaller groups of four to six. Most of the parts are interchangeable, boy with girl or girl with boy.

Contents

Desmond	7
Jumpin' Jack Flash	12
Kate and Elizabeth	17
Mind Power	23
Magic	28
Mrs. Grimsey	33
Run Cat Run	38
Rocking Horse	43
Stardust	48
Snakes Alive	53
UFO	58
Paws	63
The Word *	68

* An all-boy cast but written so that it can become an all-girl cast.

Desmond

Manager Mr. Hornby
Anne   Desmond
Marie

Mr. Hornby *works in a small firm. He is fifty-two years old and has been working in the dingy office all his working life. He is a small, pale man with a soft manner.*
The Manager *comes into the office.*
Manager   Ah Hornby. How are you?
Mr. Hornby   Fine, thank you, Mr. Samson.
Manager   Can you check through your records and see if we ever received payment from Johnson Brothers. I've just had them on the phone asking for more supplies and I've got a feeling they still owe us money.
Mr. Hornby   Yes sir.
Manager   Thank you.
Anne *has been listening to the conversation.*
Anne   What do you call him 'sir' for? I wouldn't. He's not some sort of God you know.
Mr. Hornby   Good manners don't cost anything dear.
Anne   You don't have to creep round him all the time.
Mr Hornby   I don't. Besides, it's none of your business.
Anne   I don't know how you've stuck it in here all these years. I can't stand much more of it myself.
Mr. Hornby   We all have our place in life.
Anne   I think mine's somewhere else.
Mr. Hornby   That may be.
Anne   (*noticing a bag by* Mr. Hornby's *desk*) Here, what do you carry round in that bag?
Mr. Hornby   Nothing.
Anne   Nothing?

Mr. Hornby Nothing of interest to you anyway.
Anne (*she looks in the bag*) You'd be surprised what I'm interested in.
Mr. Hornby (*closing the bag*). Chemicals.
Anne Chemicals!
Mr. Hornby Yes, chemicals. Now I must get on. (*He begins looking through a pile of papers*)
Anne What do you want chemicals for?
Mr. Hornby Ah . . . gardening mostly.
Anne Oh.

Later in the day **Anne** *is taking a message to another part of the building. She meets one of the secretaries,* **Marie**.

Anne He gives me the creeps that Hornby fella. He's not right you know.
Marie You're not kidding. I hate it when I'm in the same room. People say he's round the twist.
Anne Is he married or anything?
Marie No — who'd have him? He lives on his own in a basement flat.
Anne Does he? I bet that's a weird place.
Marie He had a party there once. You should have seen it!
Anne A party? Him!
Marie Sort of . . . he just stood watching people all the time. Nobody stayed long. I'd never go again. And his eyes — they're like pigs eyes — watery and red.
Anne Mad eyes . . .
He is mad you know. He's got a bag full of chemicals by his desk now.
Marie It doesn't surprise me. Nothing would surprise me about him.
Anne Where did you say he lived?
Marie Why?
Anne No reason.
Marie There must be a reason.
Anne No.
Marie Come on.
Anne I'm just being nosey.
Marie Are you thinking of going there?
Anne It might be a laugh. See what goes on at his house. Fancy coming?
Marie Well . . . all right.

Anne   Great. It'll be a gas seeing what he gets up to.

Meanwhile back in **Mr. Hornby**'s *office he is talking to the boss again.*

Mr. Hornby   Here's the bill.
Manager   Ah you found it; excellent.
Mr. Hornby   They have an outstanding debt, sir.
Manager   I thought so. Well done, Hornby.
Mr. Hornby   Pleasure sir.
Manager   (*looking at his watch*) Time for you to go . . . it's gone five.
Mr. Hornby   Thank you, sir.
Manager   Drop the post off for me, will you?
Mr. Hornby   Yes sir.

Later in the evening **Mr. Hornby** *is in his flat. He is mixing chemicals at the workbench.* **Marie** *and* **Anne** *have found their way there and are pressed up against the window peering through a crack in the curtains.*
Mr. Hornby *works away and suddenly looks pleased with himself.*

Mr. Hornby   My work, my work is nearly done
I've built a man to take them on
They will not laugh again at me
The man they call 'creep' Hornby
Ha . . . ha . . . ha . . .
Ha . . . ha . . . ha . . .

Suddenly from the bench there is movement. A creature resembling a human rises and totters around the room. **Mr. Hornby** *looks delighted . . .*

My plan has worked I'm ready now
To see the rest of them in hell . . .
Desmond stand still (*the creature stands*)
Desmond sit (*the creature sits*)

Mr. Hornby *gets a comb and straightens Desmond's hair and brushes bits from the clothing.*
Outside **Anne** *and* **Marie** *can't believe their eyes.*

Anne   Look at that!
Marie   I can't believe it. Can you?
Anne   We can see it. It must be true.

They are so intent on watching the creature that they don't notice **Mr. Hornby** *leave the room.*

Marie What about getting the police?
Anne We'd better do something.
Marie They'll never believe us. They'll think we're crazy.

Mr. Hornby *has crept up on them* . . .

Mr. Hornby (*taking them by surprise*) But it is true — you must believe your eyes . . .
Come in and see for yourself.
Anne (*startled*) Mr. Hornby!
Mr. Hornby Correct . . . . and Desmond. Twenty years work is sitting there waiting to meet you . . . . do come in.

* Why do you think Anne and Marie are so nosey and keen to find out about Mr. Hornby?
  What do you think happens when they are introduced to Desmond?
* Do you know any stories about monsters, robots or other creatures? Tell the class about them.
* The idea of men making creatures is a bit far-fetched, but good fun to imagine. Do you think it would be dangerous if men could make robots? What would the dangers be?
  How do you think Mr. Hornby could make sure that Desmond did no harm?
* Make a picture of Mr. Hornby.
  Start by deciding what sort of clothes he might wear and what his face might be like. Draw a picture of him and write by the side what you think he is like 'inside' . . . try to say what sort of person he is.
* Imagine Mr. Hornby has been keeping a log of his work on Desmond. Write what you think the entry might have been for the previous day. Begin . . . .
  'All my hard work is over. I will finish my man tomorrow and I think I will call him Desmond.'
* Write your own poem called *Desmond* and collect the ones from the rest of the class to make a poetry display.
* What do you think the party was like that Mr. Hornby had? Try to act out a scene where Mr. Hornby was saying hello to his guests. Try to have them looking surprised at the strangeness of the room.

* Work out the rest of the play. Act out what you think happens next. You can either perform this for the class or maybe tape record your version.
* Get into groups and discuss the details of a sequel called *The Return of Desmond.* Work out a story and decide how you are going to present it. It could be a story with music and other effects: a play; a movement and mime presentation; a collection of poems; a dance . . .

Jumpin' Jack Flash

Mum
Billy
June
Announcer

Michael
Barbara
Norman
Organiser

Billy, **June** *and their* **Mum** *are having breakfast. It is the day of the county sports competition and* **Billy** *is entered for the high jump. Because of his jumping ability he is known as 'Jumpin' Jack Flash'.*

Mum (*hearing the letter box*) Is that the post?
June I'll get it. (*She brings the letter*) It's from dad.
Mum Oh good. Open it.
June Look at the stamps. Can I have them?
Billy It's my turn.
Mum You had them last time June. It's Billy's turn. (*She tears the stamps off and gives them to* **Billy**)
Billy Thanks. These can be my lucky charm today.
Mum Let's see what dad has to say. (*She looks through the letter*) He sends his love and . . . I'm afraid he says he has to stay over another couple of months.
Billy Two months . . . he's away too long.
June That's six months now.
Mum Never mind. He has it to do. It's his job.
Billy I hate dad being away. I wish he could come and watch me this afternoon.
Mum You do your best and we'll write and tell him how you get on.
June Why can't we visit him?
Mum It'd cost a fortune. We can't afford a trip to Canada. With any luck this should be his last trip.
Billy I'll go and get ready. I'll put the stamps in my bag.

Later that day **Billy** *is at the track preparing for his event. He is talking to two of the other competitors.*

Barbara Think you'll win Billy?
Billy Don't know.
Barbara You've got a good chance.
Billy We'll see.
Michael I've pulled a muscle I think.
Barbara Excuses.
Michael No. I did it yesterday.

The **Announcer** *speaks.*

Announcer Will competitors for the high jump please go to the jumping area now. Competitors for the high jump.
Billy That's me. (*He picks his bag up and his kit spills out on the ground*)... Oh... look at that.
Barbara Nervous?
Billy No. (*He scoops his kit into his bag*)
Barbara Good luck
Billy Thanks.
Michael You'll win easy.

Billy *walks over to the jumping area and looks at the other competitors.*

Billy Hello.
Norman Hello. Are you Billy Flash?
Billy I am, yeah.
Norman I'm Norman Bates. Me and you have got the best heights this year.
Billy I know.
Norman It's between us two.
Billy Think so?
Norman Yeah. My coach reckons it'll bring out the best in me.
Billy We'll see.
Norman I only ever wear one shoe. I've never been beaten wearing one shoe. It's a sort of lucky charm for me. Are you superstitious?
Billy Not usually. I am today though.
Norman What's your luck?
Billy Stamps.
Norman Stamps?
Billy Canadian stamps.

Norman What do you do . . . stick them on the bar and aim for them?
Billy I never thought of that. I'll try it one day.

The **Organiser** *of the event comes over to sort the competitors out.*

Organiser OK now. Let's pick for jumping order. There are eight of you in and these cards are numbered.

They each choose a card.

Norman What have you got?
Billy Eight.
Norman I'm seven.
Billy All the best then.

Billy *moves away to do some warming up exercises. When he's finished he looks in his bag for the stamps. He can't find them anywhere.*

Billy Oh no. Where are those stamps? Damn. Where are they? Nothing's gone right today. I wish my dad was here to watch . . . I could do with him around.

The competition begins and each competitor has three jumps. It ends with a jump off between **Norman** *and* **Billy**.

Norman Me and you then?
Billy Looks like it.
Norman Is your charm working?
Billy Can't tell.
Norman Mine is. I cleared the bar with inches to spare last time.
Billy Did you?
Organiser Right you two. It's sudden death. We'll take the bar up half an inch and the first to clear is the winner. Understand?
Billy Yes.
Norman Who goes first?
Organiser We'll draw lots.

They do and **Norman** *is first.*

Announcer Ladies and gentlemen. Can I draw your attention to the high jump pit. We have two competitors battling it out. The bar is set at county record height and the winner will break the old record. I'm also pleased to announce a late surprise. Our sponsors have offered short scholarships to some of the winners. And the winner of the high jump competition will win a trip abroad and receive top coaching from the Canadian international team. So, all eyes on the high jump as Billy Flash and Norman Bates battle it out for a county title — and a trip to Canada.

Billy *and* **Norman** *are stunned by the announcement.*

Billy   Canada!
Norman   Canada!
Billy   My dad's there.
Norman   You've me to beat first.
Billy   I could see him . . .
Norman   Right . . . All or nothing. I fancy going to Canada just as much as you do.

Norman *jumps and fails at his first attempt. The crowd and competitors are all watching.* **Billy** *jumps and fails.*

Michael   Do you reckon he'll do it?
Barbara   Don't know. It only needs one mistake.
   (*She notices the stamps lying on the ground . . .*) Hey, what are these?
Michael   Stamps . . .
Barbara   Are they yours?
Michael   No. They must have fallen out of Billy's bag.
Barbara   Think they could help him win?
Michael   Could do.

Barbara *goes over to* **Billy** *who is about to jump.*

Barbara   Hey Billy. These yours?
Billy   Yeah. Where did you find them?
Barbara   On the ground.
Billy   Thanks, Barbara, thanks.
Announcer   Ready to jump is Billy Flash. If he makes this one he'll be our winner. Billy Flash ladies and gentlemen, better known as 'Jumpin' Jack Flash' . . .

* Are you good at any particular sport? Why is this so do you think?
* Do you have any lucky charms? Do they work for you?
* What do we mean when we say people are superstitious? Do you know anyone who is?

* Write a poem called *My Big Chance*.
* Is Billy going to win the competition?
  Work out the rest of the play as Billy prepares to jump.
* Imagine Billy does win the competition and the trip to Canada.
  Write the letter he might send explaining things to his dad.
* Write a story about Billy in Canada. His dad is with him as he competes in a competition there.
* Work out and perform the conversation Billy's mum and dad might have when his dad comes home. Mum will be pleased to see him but their talk will soon turn to the fact that the children miss him when he's away. Mum asks if he can't work nearer home.
* It will be a record if Billy clears the jump.
  What school records do you have? See if you can find out and put together your own school book of records.
* The Olympics.
  Split your class into groups of four and imagine you are teams of reporters covering the Olympic Games. Decide which event your group will be responsible for and make up stories, interviews, incidents and reports on the important events. Present your final version as a combined class effort in the form of a newspaper or radio article.

Kate and Elizabeth

Kate
Jack
Emma

Robin
Mum
Billy

Kate's *family has just moved into a rented flat in the middle of town. It is in a big old house which has been standing empty for some time.*
It is Saturday morning and the family are having breakfast.

Mum   What are you doing today Kate?
Kate   Going to Emmas — or she's coming here.
Mum   (*turning to* Billy) Billy?
Billy   Don't know.
Mum   You could help dad decorate the bathroom.
Billy   I've just remembered . . . Jack's coming round for me.
Mum   That was sudden. Who's Jack?
Billy   Emma's brother.
Mum   Is he at your school?
Billy   Yeah.
Robin   (*fed up*) I suppose I'll be the one helping dad then?
Mum   You should both help really.
Billy   He's older than me.
Robin   That makes no odds.
Billy   It does.
Robin   It doesn't.
Mum   Stop arguing.

The letter box snaps open and shut as the mail arrives.

Kate   I'll go.

She runs to the door and returns with some letters.

Mum   Bills I suppose?
Kate   Some. (*She hands them over*) One for me.
Robin   Anything for me?

17

Kate No.
Mum What are you expecting?
Robin I've written off for a job.
Mum Who's the letter from Kate?
Kate (*opening the letter and looking surprised*) Oh . . . my pen-friend.
Mum Your pen-friend? That's interesting . . .

Kate closes the letter and goes to her bedroom. It is not from her pen-friend at all. It is written on old paper in a strange handwriting.
She opens the letter and reads to herself.

Kate Dear Kate,
  Will you come to the old coaching house this morning. I have something to tell you.
  Elizabeth.

The doorbell rings. It is **Emma**. *Kate's mum sends her up to Kate's room.*

Emma Hello.
Kate Hello. Look. (*She shows her the letter*)
Emma Who's that from?
Kate I don't know.
Emma Elizabeth?
Kate I don't know anyone called Elizabeth.
Emma When did you get it?
Kate It came in the post this morning.
Emma Look at the date . . .
Kate I know!
Emma 1847!

Billy *bursts into the room.*

Billy Where's Jack, Emma?
Kate (*grabbing the letter*) What do you want?
Billy I just told you.
Emma He's on his way.
Billy What have you got there?
Kate Nothing for you.
Billy Come on. Let's have a look. (*He tries to take it*)
Kate Get off.
Billy It's a letter. It's not from your pen-friend is it. Show us . . . go on . . .
Kate No I wont.

Mum (*shouting from downstairs*) Billy.
Billy Yeah?
Mum Jack's here.
Billy Coming. (*To* **Kate**) I'll read it when you're not looking.
Kate You wont.
Billy I will.

He leaves.

Kate I hate him sometimes.
Emma He's as bad as Jack.
Kate (*looking at the letter*) 1847! That's over a hundred years ago. Are you coming with me?
Emma It's a fake.
Kate Come on Emma.
Emma Where's the coaching house anyway?
Kate It's where they're knocking all those buildings down — right in the middle of town. It's where the stage coaches used to stop in the old days.
Emma I've never heard of it.
Kate We had a lesson about it at my other school.
Emma All right then, but I think somebody's having you on.

Kate *and* **Emma** *leave the flat.*
Billy *and* **Jack** *have been waiting and follow them.*
They reach the site and have to step through dirt and rubble to get to the coaching house.

Emma This is stupid Kate.
 Somebody's playing a joke. It must be your brother.
Kate Do you think the letter came from the past?
Emma No I don't. I think it's a trick.
Kate She knew my name.
Emma So?
Kate And we've only been in the flat two weeks.
Emma You'll believe anything.

Jack *and* **Billy** *have hidden themselves behind a wall.*

Jack What are they up to?
Billy Don't know.
Jack They must be mad coming down here.
Billy They're probably looking for something.
Jack Come on I'm not waiting round here. We'll get buried under a pile of bricks.
Billy She had a letter.

Jack Big deal . . . I'm off.
Billy Hang about Jack. Just give it ten minutes.
Jack Ten minutes?
Billy Just ten.
Jack No more.

Half an hour passes and nothing happens.
Billy *and* **Jack** *have already gone.*
Kate *and* **Emma** *decide to go home.*

Emma That was a waste of time.
Kate Sorry.
Emma Somebody just wanted you to look silly.
Kate Our teacher said highwaymen used to stay here.
Emma Well they're not here now.
Kate (*still wondering*) I can't think of anybody called Elizabeth.
Emma I'll be glad when we're back home.

A week goes by and the incident is almost forgotten. On Saturday morning however another batch of mail is delivered with another letter for **Kate**. *She smuggles it to her bedroom again and reads it.*

Kate Dear Kate,
I saw you last week but I couldn't say anything because you were not alone. Please come again. It's important. There's not much time left.
Elizabeth.

Kate *leaves her room and goes quickly to the site and enters the old coaching house. She calls out into the empty rooms . . .*

Kate Hello . . . hello . . . (*Somehwere on the site a bulldozer starts up and grinds into action*) . . . hello . . . Elizabeth . . . hello . . . speak . . . I'm listening . . . hello . . . nobody's with me . . . Elizabeth . . .

Billy *has followed her from the flat and is watching. He can see her quite clearly but she can't see him. Something is happening to* **Kate**.

Billy (*amazed and afraid*) Look at that! That's not Kate. She's changing. Her hair was straight, now it's curly. (*There is fear in his voice*) She's changing, it's impossible — her clothes are different. She's wearing a long dress and a shawl. That's not Kate . . . it's somebody else! I must be seeing things.

What's happening? She's changed . . . It's somebody else . . .
it's another girl . . . Kate's changed into another girl.

The bulldozer gets slowly closer as it rattles its way towards the house . . .

Billy I'd better tell somebody. And look at that bulldozer . . . it's heading straight for the house. What's going on round here? It's mad . . . the bulldozer . . . the bulldozer . . . (*Shouting*) Look out Kate! . . . the bulldozer . . . there's no driver in it.

* What is it do you think that makes Kate believe in the letter? Would you have believed it?
* What is Emma's attitude?
* Why did Billy want to follow Kate and Emma?
* Do you think it's possible to have contact with people from the past? Is it a frightening idea? Who do you think Elizabeth is?
* What does it feel like in very old buildings? What does it sound like and what atmosphere does it have?
* Imagine Kate writes about her experience in a diary. Write what you think she would say.
* Imagine a newspaper photographer and reporter are at the demolition site making an article for the local newspaper. They bump into Kate and Billy and get their story. It is front page news.
Make the front page of the newspaper. Write a big headline, the report, and one or two supporting articles.
* Imagine you are a famous person from the past. Write a letter to someone in your class telling them of a plan they have. It might be something like Drake preparing for one of his battles or Florence Nightingale writing of her work in the hospitals. You will probably have to use your library for this or look back at some of the work you have already done in school.
* Work out and write, in small groups, what happens next. Imagine that Kate is herself again before the bulldozer knocks into the building. She hears Billy shouting and gets out of the way. They both leave the dangerous area as the bulldozer runs into a big pile of rubble and stops. Your play might begin . . .
Billy: Kate. What happened?

Kate: I don't know. I couldn't hear anything or see anything that was happening around me.
Billy: You looked different.
Kate: I know. It was Elizabeth . . .
* Work out in groups, or as a full class, your own play where one of you receives a letter from the past — or the future.

Mind Power

Mary   Tony
Arnold   Emma
Wendy

Wendy, Mary, Emma *and* Tony *are on holiday from school. They are calling for* Arnold *to see if he wants to come out with them.*

Mary   (*knocking on the door*) I bet he doesn't come.
Wendy I bet he doesn't. He's a waste of time Arnold.
Emma   He's all right. He's just different.
Wendy Is that all?

Arnold *opens the door.*

Arnold What do you lot want?
Mary   All right Arnold? Fancy coming out with us?
Arnold Where?
Mary   Don't know. Down the valley I suppose.
Arnold No thanks.
Mary   Why not?
Arnold Don't want to.
Wendy   Come on Mary. Leave him.
Mary   Come on Arnold — you never come out.
Arnold So?
Mary   What are you doing?
Arnold Reading
Wendy   I'm going. We're wasting our time here.

They turn and walk away . . .

Mary   You'll never have any friends Arnold. There's something not right about you.

Arnold *goes back inside and the group walk on.*

Tony   He's a book worm is Arnold.

Emma   He's pretty clever mind you.
Tony   I'm glad I'm thick if that's how clever makes you.
Emma   He does palm reading as well.
Mary   Palm reading?
Emma   You know. Looking at the future and things. He reckons he can see things other people can't.
Mary   That's a load of rubbish.
Emma   He says he can.
Wendy   He reads too many books.
Mary   You could make a fortune if you could see into the future.

They eventually arrive at the woods and look round for something to do.

Tony   This is a good tree Mary. Look, the branches all spread out together there. We could build a platform across.
Mary   Yeah. I suppose so. It's dead though isn't it?
Tony   Sort of. It'll be all right.
Wendy   How do we get up?
Emma   Climb!
Wendy   I know that.
Tony   I'll tie this rope over that big branch and we can make a ladder.
Emma   This tree is just right.
Mary   Go on then Tony. Climb up and sling that rope over.
Tony   OK. (*He climbs easily and drops the rope*)
Mary   Right Emma. You go up next and me and Wendy will collect some wood to make a platform.

Mary *organises the wood and they build a platform. Eventually they are all settled in the tree wondering what to do next.*

Mary   It's good up here isn't it?
Wendy   Not bad.
Tony   You can see our school.
Wendy   Have we done all this just to sit and look at our school?
Emma   (*discovering something*) There's a big hole in the tree here.
Wendy   It's dead, that's why. I hope it doesn't fall down.
Mary   Trees like this don't fall down.
Emma   It's full of stones.
Tony   Stones?
Emma   Yeah, look. (*she pulls a few out*)

Tony Anything else in there?
Emma I don't think so.
Tony Have a look.

Emma *pulls all the stones out and eventually finds a piece of paper.*

Emma Look at this!
Tony What is it?
Emma (*opening it*) A map.
Mary No!
Wendy It's a joke. Chuck it away. Somebody's having us on.
Tony Who knew we were coming here?
Wendy Somebody else might use this tree.
Tony So who's to say it's not their map, and they know something we don't?
Mary Let's have a look. (**Emma** *hands it to her*)
Wendy What does it say?
Mary I don't know. It's in code. I can't read it.
Wendy (*scoffing*) This is kid's stuff.
Mary Have a look yourself. Tell us what you think.
Wendy I can't understand it. It looks like a map of these woods but I can't understand the writing.
Tony No. It's foreign isn't it?
Mary If we could work out what it said we might find something.
Wendy (*mocking*) Don't tell me . . . treasure . . .
Mary If you think it's a joke Wendy you can go home. Nobody's making you stay.
Wendy You make me tired Mary.
Tony I know who could read it.
Emma So do I . . . Arnold.
Mary Yeah, he could. Let's go and get him.

Tony *goes back to* **Arnold**'s *house and persuades him to come down.* **Arnold** *isn't very keen though.*

Arnold (*climbing the tree*) I hope I can get down once I'm up. I don't like getting dirty.
Tony Come on Arnold it's easy, don't be so useless.
Arnold I hate climbing. I hate messing about.

He reaches the platform.

Mary All right Arnold? Look. (*She gets the map*) What do you reckon this is?
Arnold What?

Mary A map.
Arnold I can see that, but so what?
Emma We found it.
Mary In this tree — here. (*She shows him*)
Arnold Somebody must have put it there.
Wendy Brilliant Arnold!
Mary We can't read it Arnold — can you?
Arnold It's easy, it's a code.
Mary Go on then.
Arnold It's a back to front alphabet. X=A. Piece of cake.
Mary Oh yeah? Come on then, read . . .
Arnold Just a minute.
(*He works it all out*) It says. Take eight paces west from the foot of this tree and start digging.
Mary And . . . ?
Arnold That's all.
Wendy This is a big joke — and nobody's laughing.
Mary Come on then. Let's get digging.
Arnold Wait a minute, there's something else.
Emma What Arnold?
Arnold (*moving to the hole in the tree*) I reckon if we reach down into this hole even further, we'll find something else . . . something valuable.

* Do you feel like Wendy — that it's all a big joke?
* What do you think Arnold finds as he reaches down into the tree?
* Do you believe in this sort of power — the power to see things as Arnold believes he can?
* Do you believe in palm reading and reading tea-leaves or packs of cards? Is it dangerous to get involved in this sort of thing?
* If the code is X=A, write the coded message which was written on the paper. Make up a code of your own and send a message to a friend — see if anyone else can work it out.
* Write in story form what happens after Arnold reaches into the tree saying that he senses that there is something else in there — something valuable.
* Draw a map of an area of ground that you know and make it into a treasure map. Make up a riddle that has to be solved before the map can mean anything to anybody.

* Write as much as you can about Arnold. Say what you think he does in his spare time; how he dresses, what he likes to eat, where he goes, what he's like at school.
  Draw a picture of him or find a suitable picture and stick it next to your description.
* Work out and act the part of the play as the people count eight paces and start digging. Decide what they find and what happens as a result.
* In groups of four or five (or if possible the whole class) prepare and produce a play called *Power* which shows how one person's special power helps others. Some types of power which might help you get started are,
  Muscle power; running power; brain power; climbing power; swimming power; people power.
  To start with you'll have a situation where some of you are in need of help and others have the power to help you.

Magic

Alex
Beverley
Mum
Dad

Leo (the Magician)
Rosemary (his assistant)
Compere

Alex *and* Beverley *are getting ready to go to the local pantomime.* Mum *is chasing everybody round.*

Mum   Come on now. We're going to be late.
Dad   Coming.
Alex   I can't find any socks.
Mum   Your drawer — where else?
Alex   I can't see any.
Mum   You haven't looked properly. Get a move on.
Beverley   (*reading the ticket*) There's a magician at the pantomime.
Dad   I didn't know they had magicians at pantomimes.
Beverley   That's what it says on the tickets. (*She shows him*)
Dad   (*looking*) If it says so it says so. I just hope he's good. There's nothing worse than a bad magician.
Alex   (*coming into the room*) Found them. Under my bed . . .
Mum   About time. And what were they doing under your bed?
Alex   I don't know.
Dad   I'm ready. Let's go.

They all hurry out.
Backstage at the pantomime the performers are getting ready.
The **Magician** *and his assistant are nervous.*

Magician   Rosemary, where's my cape?
Rosemary   Here. (*She hands it to him*)
Magician   Thank you. My hat?
Rosemary   Here. You seem tense tonight.
Magician   I'm worried about the trick.
Rosemary   Which trick?

Magician The big one. The disappearing girl.
Rosemary Why?
Magician I don't know. I just have a funny feeling about it.
Rosemary There haven't been any problems before.
Magician I know, but there's always a first time.
Rosemary There's no point worrying now — the show starts in five minutes.
Magician I know.

Meanwhile the family have entered and taken their seats.

Dad Let's hope it's good.
Mum It usually is.
Beverley Can I go up if they ask for someone to go on stage?
Dad You can try.
Alex I want to as well.
Mum You can both try.
Alex I bet we don't get picked.
Beverley Julie Graham got picked last year.
Mum Let's just wait and see, and stop talking for a bit. It's like organising an expedition getting you two out.

The Magician is still worried.

Magician My wand Rosemary. Where's my wand?
Rosemary You had it a minute ago.
Magician I know but it's gone. Where did I put it?
Rosemary You really are a bundle of nerves tonight.
Magician I can't go on without it.
Rosemary Stay calm.
Magician It's nowhere.
Rosemary You could perform without it couldn't you?
Magician It wouldn't be right. (*Noticing the box*) Have you checked the box?
Rosemary Yes.
Magician Is it all right?
Rosemary Perfectly all right.

There is a knock on the door and a voice tells the **Magician** *he's on next.*

Magician That's our call.
Rosemary Come on. Let's get the performance done. I'll be glad when tonight's over.

They move to the side of the stage and the compere introduces the act to the audience.

29

Compere Ladies and gentlemen, boys and girls. Tonight we interrupt the pantomime to bring you the famous Leo. Leo has performed throughout the land and has a fine reputation. He will show you some amazing tricks and will perform a breath-taking disappearing act before your very eyes.
Leo the magician . . .

The audience clap as he enters with **Rosemary**. *He performs some opening tricks and eventually everything goes quiet as he introduces his disappearing trick.*

Magician For my next trick I require the services of a young lady from the audience.

Lots of hands go up — including **Beverley's**.

Magician I will ask my assistant to come amongst you and choose a girl who will enter this box here and on the count of three will disappear.

Rosemary *walks up the aisle towards* **Beverley** *and* **Alex**.

Beverley I hope it's me.

Rosemary *stops and looks at* **Beverley**.

Rosemary Yes. Come on then. What's your name?
Beverley Beverley.

Beverley *gets up and walks away with the assistant.*

Rosemary Come on. Are you nervous?
Beverley No.
Rosemary Good. There's nothing to worry about.
Magician My assistant has chosen a girl. I see her coming now. Give her a big hand.

Beverley *climbs on the stage looking very pleased with herself.*

Mum Look at her . . . doesn't she look lost on stage . . .?
Dad She does.
Alex I don't know why she gets picked for everything.
Magician Ladies and gentlemen. You see this box is completely empty. There are no panels, no hidden doors. I will ask Beverley to step in and I will fasten the box and count to three. On the count of three she will disappear. Silence please . . .

He helps **Beverley** *into the box and* **Rosemary** *closes the lid.*

Magician   Now then. Beverley be still. (*There is a roll on the drums*) One . . . two . . . three . . . (*The cymbals crash*) (**Rosemary** *opens the lid and the box is empty. The* **Magician** *whispers to* **Rosemary**) . . . So far so good . . . (*He speaks to the audience*) I will now bring Beverley back. Close the lid please. (**Rosemary** *closes it*) Beverley, return to the box. One . . . two . . . three . . . (**Rosemary** *rushes to open the box and is shocked to find it is still empty. She closes the box again and the* **Magician** *repeats his line*) Beverley, return to the box. One . . . two . . . three . . . (**Rosemary** *again opens the box and still it is empty. The audience begin to get worried.*)
Mum   Beverley!
Dad   What's he doing, the fool?
Mum   He can't get her back . . .
Magician   Quiet everyone please.

There is a long silence.

Beverley return to the box. One . . . two . . . three . . . .

* Why do you think the magician is feeling nervous about the performance?
* Do you believe in magic or is it all a clever trick?
* Do you ever have the feeling that things are going to go wrong? Is there any explanation for this?
* It's not really possible for people to disappear — so why do you think disappearing acts are so interesting to people?
* Houdini was a man famous for performing incredible escapes. Try to find out something about him from books in your library. Write an account of some of his most famous escapes.
* Write an ending for the play. Begin where the magician ends saying, 'Beverley return to the box. One, two, three . . . '
Get together in groups and act out the play.
Let's make it so that Beverley returns safe and sound.
* With a friend, work out the conversation Rosemary and the magician have the following night when they are preparing to perform the trick again. There will be more interest than ever now and reporters will be amongst the crowds gathered in the hall.
Imagine you are a newspaper reporter and write a report on what happens for your newspaper.

* Why do you think we have entertainers?
  People like to go to shows, pantomimes, plays, films, concerts . . . Do you think pretending is as interesting as real things?
  Either write an account of an entertainment you remember or write a story called *The Entertainer.*
* If you were an entertainer what sort would you like to be? Draw a picture of how you would like to look.
* Prepare and perform your own magic show. There are many books which explain simple tricks and maybe you could invent your own disappearing act.
  You could have several people being magicians with a person to introduce each one. You could also include comedians, impersonators, dancers and singers . . .

Mrs. Grimsey

Sarah 　　　　　　　　Jennifer
Mrs. Grimsey 　　　　　Mum

It is Saturday afternoon. **Sarah** *is in the house and has nothing to do.*

Mum　What are you doing this afternoon?
Sarah　Nothing.
Mum　Nothing! Why nothing?
Sarah　I don't know. I'm bored.
Mum　I can think of plenty for you to do.
Sarah　I'm all right. I'm not worried about it.
Mum　I don't know about that. (*She thinks for a moment*) You can go and see if Mrs. Grimsey has any shopping she wants doing.
Sarah　Oh no!
Mum　Oh yes. She's old and can't get out on her own. Go round and ask if she has any jobs.
Sarah　Mum!
Mum　Don't mum me. You go and see if you can help . . . It'll do you good. We have to help neighbours, especially old ones.
Sarah　I don't want to.
Mum　Do as you're told.

Sarah *complains a bit, but goes round to* **Mrs. Grimsey**'s *house and knocks on the door.*

Mrs. Grimsey　Hello.
Sarah　Hello Mrs. Grimsey. Have you any shopping you want me to do? My mum sent me to ask.
Mrs. Grimsey　Oh, that's kind. Yes please. Come in a minute. I could do with some bread and sugar and some sausages. It's very nice of you. Come in . . .
Sarah *enters*. . . Now then. I think you'll get it all in the grocers. It's very nice. Here, I'll write a list.

Sarah   Don't worry about a list. I can remember.
Mrs. Grimsey   Are you sure? Half a pound of sausages, a loaf of bread and a bag of sugar.
Sarah   Right.
Mrs. Grimsey   Oh, and some orange juice Sarah. Yes — some orange juice. (*Taking her purse*) Here's some money, and you'll need a bag.
Sarah   It's all right. I can manage without a bag.
Mrs. Grimsey   Are you sure?
Sarah   I'm sure.

Sarah *leaves and goes to the shop. She arrives back about twenty minutes later.* **Mrs. Grimsey** *takes her into the living room.*

Mrs. Grimsey   That was quick. It's a big help dear. You sit down and I'll make a drink of orange for you.
Sarah   It's all right Mrs. Grimsey. I'm not thirsty.
Mrs. Grimsey   You deserve it after being so kind. And a biscuit. Have one of my special biscuits. I'll go and get them. (*She goes to the kitchen*)

Sarah *looks round the room and notices how dark it is. It is also pretty cold and damp feeling. There are old fashioned photographs everywhere and a clock ticks loudly on the mantlepiece. The chair she is sitting on is hard and rough. She can hear* **Mrs. Grimsey** *messing with the orange juice. Suddenly there is a loud banging on the ceiling.* **Sarah** *jumps and feels frightened. The banging continues and is followed by a sort of groan. More knocking and groaning comes from upstairs and* **Sarah** *is ready to run out when* **Mrs. Grimey** *returns.*

Mrs. Grimsey   Here we are. Orange juice and my special biscuits. You'll stay for a bit will you? You aren't rushing off?
Sarah   Well . . .
Mrs. Grimsey   If I'm not being greedy, can I ask you to do me another favour. It's tomorrow you see — can you come tomorrow and . . .
Sarah   I don't know about tomorrow. I think I might be going out.
Mrs. Grimsey   It wont take a minute. I want you to help me move some furniture around in the bedroom . . .

Later that day **Sarah** *is talking to her mum.*

Sarah   It's dead spooky. I'm not going there again.

Mum Don't be silly. Old people are different that's all. There's nothing spooky about them.
Sarah I heard noises. Banging and groaning.
Mum Banging and groaning?
Sarah Coming from upstairs. That place is haunted.
Mum Don't talk silly. That was probably Mr. Grimsey.
Sarah Mr. Grimsey?
Mum Yes. He's been poorly for ages now. I think he more or less stays in bed all the time.
Sarah Oh.
Mum You're making something out of nothing.
Sarah So would you if you'd been there on your own.
Mum Jennifer can go with you tomorrow.
Sarah Tomorrow!
Mum I thought you said she asked you to help move some furniture?
Sarah She did but . . .
Mum But what?
Sarah I don't want to go there again mum.
Mum You're being silly.
Sarah No I'm not.
Mum I said you are. You and Jennifer will go and help Mrs. Grimsey for half an hour. It's not a lot to ask.

The next day **Jennifer** *and* **Sarah** *are waiting outside* **Mrs. Grimsey's** *house.*

Sarah I'm warning you. There's something not right about this place. . . . and Mrs. Grimsey.
Jennifer Mum said you were being stupid.
Sarah (*knocking on the door*) I'm not. There are noises in here.
Jennifer It's Mr. Grimsey . . .

Mrs. Grimsey *opens the door.*

Mrs. Grimsey Ah, here you are . . . and your sister . . . It's good of you to come. I've been expecting you.

They all go into the living room.

Mrs. Grimsey Sit down a minute. I'm just doing some baking.

She goes into the kitchen . . .
The noises begin again. There is banging and tapping and an even stranger groaning noise. **Sarah** *and* **Jennifer** *are both very worried.*

Sarah I told you.

Jennifer   Shut up Sarah. It's Mr. Grimsey. It must be.
Mrs. Grimsey   (*returning*) Right now I'm ready. It shouldn't take long. I just want to re-arrange the bedroom a bit now that Mr. Grimsey has gone into the home.
Sarah   Home?
Mrs. Grimsey   Yes love. He's been really ill you know. It's best — and I can visit him whenever I like. It reminds me of him the way it is. I want to move it round a bit and drive out the bad memories.

* Why doesn't Sarah want to go to Mrs. Grimsey's in the first place?
* What do you think the noises are? Is there some obvious explanation?
* What sort of things in a house make it seem different, uncomfortable or spooky?
* Have you any elderly neighbours near you? Do you try and help them?
* Draw a picture of the inside of Mrs. Grimsey's house.
* Write a description of Mrs. Grimsey. Say what her clothes are like, her hair, her skin, her hands, her eyes, her teeth, her voice and her walk.
* Do you know of any stories or legends about strange happenings? Perhaps you could look for some in your library. Tell the class about them.
* Continue the play by working out what happens when Sarah and Jennifer go upstairs to help move the furniture. Look back to the second question before you begin.
* What noises and sounds frighten people and why? Discuss them in groups and try to make some of these sounds and record them if you can.
* Use this plot and write a play called *Home is Where the Ghost Is*.
    a) a young boy or girl goes to stay in an old house
    b) during the night the lights flash on and off
    c) the next day the telephone is out of order
    d) in the evening there is a blizzard and the house is cut off
    e) just before the television breaks down there is a news flash giving warning of strange happenings in that area
    f) at eleven o'clock something unexpected happens.

If you decide to perform your play you could use some of your sound effects from the question before last to help give the play its haunted atmosphere.

Run Cat Run

Pamela
Sarah
Lisa
Mark

William
'Cat'
Two men

Pamela, Sarah, Lisa, Mark and **William** *are walking along a deserted beach. They have lost their friend,* **Catherine** — *they call her* **'Cat'** *for short.*

Lisa Cat . . . Cat . . .
Pamela We're wasting our time. She's gone.
Lisa Where has she gone?
Sarah She can't have gone far. There's nowhere to go.
Mark I'm fed up. I've had enough of this.
Lisa Keep quiet. You're always fed up.
Mark Well.
Pamela You get water from a well.
Lisa (*shouting*) Cat . . . Cat . . .
Sarah I wonder if she's hiding?
Pamela No.
Mark She might be.
Lisa Mrs. Hughes'll murder us if we go back without her.
Sarah She might have gone back already.
Mark I think she's wasting our time.
Pamela Stop talking so much. You're not coming again Mark.
Mark I'd like to see you stop me.
Pamela Would you?
Mark Yeah, I would.
Lisa Shut up you two. You're no use to anybody.
Sarah (*noticing* **William** *who hasn't said a word*) What's wrong William?
William Nothing.
Sarah Why are you quiet?
William I'm scared.

Sarah Scared . . . why?
William I don't know. I can feel something.
Sarah What can you feel?
William Something.
Mark I feel something — frozen I think you call it.
William Something's going on. There's danger on this beach.
Sarah Don't start talking like that.
William There is — I can feel it.
Lisa What's he on about?
Sarah He says he can feel danger.
William Danger.
Pamela Let's go then.
Mark Suits me. I've had enough.
Lisa What about Cat? We can't leave her . . .
William She's in trouble.
Lisa What trouble?
Pamela How do you know? How can you tell?
Mark William looks rough to me.
Pamela He does, yeah. He's as white as a sheet.
Mark He looks frightened stiff.
Pamela What's he looking at?
William Over there. (*He points across the beach*) A boat . . .
Sarah Let's get out of sight — hide.

They scatter and hide behind a breakwater.

William I think that's Cat on the boat.

They strain their eyes to see a boat in the distance.

Sarah We'll wait till they're on the beach.
Mark This is a job for the police. Let's go and ring them.
Pamela Let's ring your skinny neck.
Mark This is nothing to do with us.
Pamela It is if those fellas have got Cat.
Mark Rubbish. You watch too much television Things like that don't happen in real life. It's children's hour stuff.
Lisa We'll soon know. They've beached the boat.
William It looks like they're carrying shovels.
Sarah Let's run round the back of those dunes and get nearer.
Lisa Good idea.
Pamela Yeah. Come on. You can stay here if you like Mark . . . or go back. We don't need you.
Mark Don't worry. I'll come. I'll play games with you.

Lisa (*grabbing his hair*) This isn't a game.
Mark All right . . . all right . . . let go.
Sarah Come on then.

They move off and creep down behind a breakwater further up the beach.

Lisa It is Cat, look.
Sarah She looks scared to me.
Pamela What can we do?
William She's in danger.
Lisa We could run at them.
Mark I said we should have got the police.

Two men *are walking up the beach with* **Cat** . . .

1st Man Right then little girl. About here I think.
2nd Man Are you sure the tide comes up this far?
1st Man Look at the tide mark — up beyond that breakwater . . .
2nd Man If you say so.
1st Man Start digging.
2nd Man There are two shovels.
1st Man Start digging.

Back with the group.

Lisa Look at that!
Pamela What are they going to do?
Mark This is stupid. I'm going to walk up and ask them what's happening.
Lisa Move and I'll flatten you.
Mark Oh yeah? You . . .
Lisa Yeah me . . . If they see us they might clear off again — and we might never find Cat.
William There is danger about you know. I can smell it.
Sarah If we could get Cat's attention she could run. We could stick together then.
Lisa When the men turn away, you stand up and wave.
Pamela Right.
Sarah Don't let them see you.
Pamela I wont.
Mark (*scoffing*) Very dramatic!
Lisa I'll see you when this is sorted out.
Mark See me now, I would. Why wait?

The **two men** *turn away.* **Pam** *stands and catches* **Cat***'s attention. She looks around her and starts to run. . .*

The group stand up and start yelling.

Lisa   Come on — quick.
Pamela   Run Cat . . .
Sarah   They've seen us.

The **two men** *see* **Cat** *running . . .*

Pamela   Run Cat run . . . .

* Have you ever felt like William — that there was danger about?
* Why is Mark not taking the concern of the others seriously? Do you think he's trying to hide his own feelings or does he really think they're being too dramatic?
* Have you ever dreamed that you were running away from somebody or something? Tell of your dream and the thoughts you had.
* Imagine Cat writes the day's happenings in her diary that night. Write what happens before we join them; how she got involved with the men in the first place and how she got separated from the group. It might begin . . . .
  'It was a nice sunny day so I decided to walk along the beach. I thought I saw something floating in the water . . . '
* Write the conversation Mark and Lisa have when they get back to safe surroundings. It could begin . . .
  Lisa: Well?
  Mark: Well what?
  Lisa: I said I'd see you when everything was sorted out.
* Write a poem called *Low Tide.* Make a class collection and tape record them or display them.
* Work out an ending for the play. Make sure you decide who the men are and why Cat was with them. It could, of course, have been quite innocent.
* Write and draw a cartoon strip story of something that has happened to you on a beach.
* *The Cave.*
  Use this outline and work out a play to perform:
  a) a group of young people have a metal detector and are combing the beach
  b) one of them suggests they look in a cave
  c) they find a few bits and pieces and eventually something which is very big and solid
  d) one of them goes back for help

e) the others dig on and are interrupted by a local man who tells them it used to be a smuggler's cave
f) another man comes along and says they might have discovered an unexploded bomb.

Rocking Horse

Gran
Christine
Robert

Mum
Removal Man 1
Removal Man 2

Grandma Burton *is moving from her own house to live with her grandchildren,* **Christine** *and* **Robert**. *She is not keeping many bits of furniture but one thing she is bringing is the old rocking horse which* **Christine** *used to play on as a young girl.*

Gran (*instructing the removal men*) Be careful now, he's very sensitive.
Removal Man 1 Where do you want it lady?
Gran In the bedroom please.
Removal Man 1 Upstairs?
Gran Yes. Be careful though, he can't afford to have any more of his paint chipped. And look at his mane . . . it's all dropping out.
Removal Man 1 Come on Frank. You take the back legs. I'll take his head (*They lift*)
Removal Man 2 Right ho.
Gran I'll leave you to it.

She leaves . . .

Removal Man 2 Stroll on! All this for a rocking horse.

They begin to climb the stairs.

Removal Man 1 Stop talking Frank. I don't like the way this thing's looking at me.
Removal Man 2 Looking at you?
Removal Man 1 His glass eye's fixed on me good and proper.
Removal Man 2 Mind he doesn't bite your hand.

Christine *comes in from school.*

Christine Gran . . . Gran . . .
Mum (*coming into the hall*) Quietly . . . you'll wake the dead.

43

Christine   Has Gran brought the horse?
Mum   Gran's in the kitchen.
Christine   Where's the horse?
Mum   Christine!
Christine   Upstairs? (*She runs upstairs*)
Mum   (*calling after her*) What's so special about that horse anyway?

Robert *comes in from school.*

Robert   Hello mum.
Mum   Hello Robert . . . I'll gag your sister one of these days.
Robert   What's the matter with her now?
Mum   Anybody'd think she was a three year old . . . going potty over a rocking horse.

Christine *comes to the top of the stairs.*

Christine   It's here mum, in my bedroom.

The removal men pass her.

Removal Man 2   Excuse me love.
Removal Man 1   Is that your horse?
Christine   Yes.
Removal Man 1   He's had his eye on me!
Christine   Has he?
Removal Man 1   He's happy enough now though.

The removal men leave and **Robert** *joins* **Christine** *in the bedroom.*

Robert   It looks tatty to me.
Christine   Be quiet.
Robert   And small. It used to be bigger than that.
Christine   He's perfect.
Robert   Could do with a paint.
Christine   No he couldn't. How would you like to be painted.
Robert   Quite a bit if I was made out of wood.
Christine   He's as real as you and me.
Robert   Funny.
Christine   Come in here tonight if you don't believe me.
Robert   Are you nuts?
Christine   There's one way to find out. Come in at nine o'clock.

Gran *enters. . .*

Gran Hello you two.
Christine Gran . . . thanks for bringing the horse.
Robert Hello Gran.
Gran Hello Robert. (*To* **Christine**) You used to ride till I thought you'd wear him out when you were little. He looks pleased to see you.
Christine He is. He'll be happy now.
Robert (*leaving*) I'll see you later.
Christine Don't forget Rob — nine o'clock.
Robert You're joking. (*He leaves*)
Gran What's all that about?
Christine Robert's being awkward as usual.
Gran You two shouldn't argue so much.

Later in the evening **Robert** *is in his bedroom.*

Robert She must be joking. Girls are always the same . . . how can a lump of wood be real? I'm not going — what's the point? (*He waits for a while and then looks at his watch*) Nine o'clock now. I suppose she'll be feeding it sugar lumps or something — bedding it down for the night. Still it'd be a laugh to see her doing it. I think I'll go and have a laugh . . . yeah, why not?

He gets up and goes to **Christine**'s *room.*

Christine I knew you'd come.
Robert No you didn't because I've only just decided. I've told you I think you're nuts.
Christine Why did you come then?
Robert A laugh, what else?
Christine You wont be laughing in a minute. Jump on.
Robert What?
Christine Jump on. Barnaby'll take you for a ride.
Robert On that rocking horse?
Christine Yes.
Robert I'm not a kid . . .
Christine If you get on and ride he'll take you wherever you like.
Robert Oh yeah — well I'll go to China then! Ha. Do you think I'm as daft as you are?
Christine All right, we'll both get on.
Robert No chance.
Christine Come on. (*She gets on*) Come on coward.

45

Robert   Coward?
Christine   Yes. Climb on.
Robert   No.
Christine   All right then. I'll go on my own. I think I'll go to Julie's in Plumtree Drive.
Robert   Plumtree Drive! That's only round the corner.
Christine   It's far enough to start with. Come on Barnaby.

She begins to ride the horse backwards and forwards. She gets faster and faster. **Robert** *gets dizzy watching and the whole room seems to spin. He rubs his eyes so he can focus better and eventually he opens them to find* **Christine** *and the horse gone . . . After a moment* **Robert** *is startled by a tapping on the door.*

Robert   Who is it?
Gran   It's only me, Gran . . . can I come in?

* Why does Robert think that the horse has got smaller?
* Why does he go to see Christine at nine o'clock? Why can't he resist?
* Does anybody else in the play think that the rocking horse is a little bit real?
* Have you any objects or toys which are 'real' to you? Did you have them when you were younger? What were they?
* Imagine one of the removal men keeps a diary. He has been struck by how the rocking horse kept looking at him. Write the entry for his diary on that day. You could begin . . . 'The day started as usual, breakfast and then down the depot to pick up the van. A small job to start with, moving a few bits for an old lady. One of these bits was a rocking horse . . .'
* This is a story which couldn't really happen except in your imagination. Imagine, though, that you had the rocking horse and could go anywhere you liked. Write the story of where you go and what hapens to you.
* With a partner, act out the conversation Robert has with Gran as he lets her in at the end of the play. Gran might begin by asking where Christine is. You could include other people and work out what happens next.
* There are a number of stories about toys and animals which come to life. See if you can find any in your library and read them. One of the most well-known ones is *Pinocchio*.

* Imagine the rocking horse has a chance to talk and starts a conversation with Christine's mum or dad one night when they are alone in the house. Write or act out the conversation.
* Make your classroom or drama room into a young person's bedroom. Imagine that at certain times the toys and games come to life. Work out a story which shows this happening. Spend some time talking about what toys there will be and how they will speak and move.

Stardust

Sally
Ben
Mr. Stardust

Rebecca
Ruth
Rob

Sally, Ben, Rebecca, Ruth and Rob are on an international youth camp. They have left the camp site and gone down into the seaside town to look round.

Sally What do you fancy doing?
Ben Swim?
Rebecca I wouldn't mind a swim.
Rob I want to go on the fairground first.
Sally Good idea.
Rebecca Fairgrounds are always the same — they cost a lot of money.
Rob We don't have to spend much.
Ruth Let's go on the pier.
Rob There's nothing on the pier.
Ruth There's amusements.
Rob That's a real waste of money.
Ruth We'll split up then. Who wants to go on the pier?
Rebecca It's best to stick together Ruth. We can do everything anyway. We've got plenty of time.
Rob Right, we'll start with the fairground.
Rebecca Come on Ruth.
Ruth All right.
Ben Can we go for a swim after?
Sally Course we can.
Rebecca I'll swim Ben.
Ben OK.

They can see the outline of the fairground in the distance. They walk towards it. Rowdy music is playing and there are the sounds of rifle shots, waltzers, space rides, big dippers and dodgems.

Sally   Magic!
Ben   Yeah. Come on. Let's go on the dipper. Look at it!

They see the cars speed down the slope and up the other side. The riders scream.

Rebecca   I couldn't stand that.
Ruth   Let's go on the waltzer.
Rob   I'll go on with you.
Sally   (*noticing a small building and reading the notice*) Mr. Stardust...
Ben   What?
Sally   Look at that there. There's somebody dressed up as a wizard. It says Mr. Stardust.
Ben   So what?
Sally   I fancy going to see. Coming?
Ben   (*looking at the fairground*) What about all this?
Sally   There's plenty of time. Come on.
Ben   All right then. (*To the others*) Anybody coming to see?
Rob   Mr. Stardust! No chance. I'm going on the waltzer.
Ruth   We'll meet up later. Rob and me are going on the waltzer.
Rebecca   I'll come with you Ben. See what it's all about.
Ben   Come on then.

Ben, Rebecca *and* **Sally** *move over to the hut.*

Mr. Stardust   Hello, hello, hello...
Sally   Hello. What do you do?
Mr. Stardust   This, my dear, is my house of magic. The place where dreams come true.
Sally   Oh yeah? Not very busy are you?
Mr. Stardust   That's because people don't believe in magic. Those who do are rewarded.
Rebecca   How much is it?
Mr. Stardust   For the small sum of one pound you can be sprinkled with glittering stardust and have your biggest wish come true.
Ben   A pound!
Sally   I'm not surprised you're not busy.
Mr. Stardust   A pound for a dream! A pound to see your dreams come true. It's the best value for money on the fairground.
Sally   Can you wish for anything?
Mr. Stardust   Anything — within reason. I can't allow you to wish the sea would dry up or sand catch fire. But I can give

you a chance to fulfil your dreams, or realize your ambition.
Sally   Oh yeah . . . ?
Ben   (*To* **Sally**) He's a nutter.
Rebecca   He's got a nerve. A pound to have dust thrown at you. I'll do that for nothing Sally.
Ben   It's daylight robbery.

They move away slightly so that **Mr. Stardust** *can't hear them.*

Sally   What do you think?
Ben   We just said what we think.
Rebecca   Come on. He's a waste of time.
Sally   Not so fast.
Ben   You're not thinking of wasting your money on this?
Sally   I might be.
Rebecca   You're mad.
Sally   We could share the cost.
Ben   Who gets the wish?
Sally   It doesn't matter who gets the wish.
Rebecca   I don't want to wish . . . It's embarassing.
Sally   What about you Ben?
Ben   If you ask me it's a waste of money. I feel stupid even standing here. The others'll think we're mad. There's nobody else trying it. He's a fake. He must be.
Rebecca   You'd better do the wishing Sally.
Ben   What are you going to wish for anyway?
Sally   I can't tell you that.
Ben   Why not?
Sally   Wishes don't work if you tell people.
Rebecca   How will we know if you get your wish or not?
Sally   You wont.
Ben   Big deal! Come on Sally. This is getting dafter. I'm going.
Sally   Hang on Ben. Come on, just for a laugh. He'll let us all in . . .

Ben *looks at* **Rebecca** *and they reluctantly agree.*
They return to **Mr. Stardust.**

Mr. Stardust   Ah . . . you made a wise decision.
Sally   Can we all come in?
Mr. Stardust   Who is having the wish?
Sally   Me.
Mr. Stardust   Very well. But you must be quiet and still and remember; you must believe. If you don't believe the stardust will have no power.

Sally Right.
Mr. Stardust Come then.

He takes them into the hut. It is painted black and has dim coloured lights shining. There are silver painted stars hanging from the ceiling. **Rebecca** *and* **Ben** *are told to sit at the back.* **Sally** *steps forward and sits in a red velvet chair.* **Mr. Stardust** *stands still for a moment and then goes to a box and takes out a jar. He takes the top off the jar and pours some of the green dust into his hand. He gives* **Sally** *a card to read from.*

Sally (*reading*) Will you sprinkle me with stardust?
Mr. Stardust Make your wish . . . think it, don't speak it.

Sally *is silent for a moment . . .*

Mr. Stardust Would you hurt anyone?
Sally No.
Mr. Stardust Would you cheat anyone?
Sally No.
Mr. Stardust Would you always try to be truthful?
Sally Yes.
Mr. Stardust Very well then . . .
  (*He sprinkles stardust over* **Sally**)
  The dust of the star
  the air of the night
  the lid off the jar
  and wishes take flight

  You can see whatever you want to see
  be whatever you want to be
  If you must . . .
  Close your eyes and be sprinkled with
  Stardust . . . .

Mr. Stardust *throws the dust into the air and it lands in green speckles all over* **Sally**. *Her eyes are closed tight and she is wishing hard.*
She opens her eyes after a moment and gets out of the chair. Everyone is watching her.

Ben (*whispering*) Is that it?
Mr. Stardust Hush. Don't break the spell. Can't you see your friend is still in the grip of the wish?

Sally *slowly walks outside.*
Ben *and* **Rebecca** *follow her.*

Ben Come on then. It's partly my money she's wishing with.
Rebecca Any good Sally?
Sally I'll tell you in a minute . . .

She walks on and they follow . . .

* Do you believe that wishes come true?
* Do you think Sally gets her wish? What do you think it was? What would your wish be?
* Why don't Rebecca and Ben want to make the wish?
* Do you think it would be dangerous if people could have their wishes come true?
  Notice that Mr. Stardust makes Sally say that she wont harm or cheat anyone, or be untruthful.
* Imagine Mr. Stardust needs another magic rhyme to go with his wish making. Write it for him.
* Write the story of what happens next. You can include new places and new people if you like.
* Draw a picture of Mr. Stardust inside his room. Use some of the descriptions from the play to help you get started.
* Imagine a television producer brings a team down to the fairground to interview Mr. Stardust. Show what happens by either writing a play or acting out the scene. There will be cameras, microphones, lights and lots of questions for Mr. Stardust.
* Act out what happens as Ruth and Rob wander round the fairground together. Imagine they are attracted to one of the side-shows (perhaps a fortune teller or a wrestling match) and decide to take part.
* Get into small groups and talk about some of the wishes you have had or would like to have come true. Work out the plot of a play called *The Wish*. Each person could write his own part and the final script could be rehearsed and performed as a short play.

Snakes Alive

Simon Teacher
Colin Melanie
Lucy Keeper

A class of children are on a school trip, visiting the zoo. Simon, Colin, Melanie and Lucy are together.

Melanie I fancy seeing the tigers.
Colin All right. Where are they?
Melanie (*looking at a map of the zoo*) Next to the cafe . . . that's . . . well it should be left, down this path here.
Colin What time's feeding?
Melanie Three o'clock. What's the time now?
Lucy Five to three.
Melanie Come on then. We'd better get a move on.
Lucy What time do they feed the sea-lions?
Melanie No idea. Sea-lions are boring anyway.
Lucy No they're not.
Melanie You go and see them if you want. We'll see the tigers. Are you ready Colin?
Colin Yeah, I'm ready. What about you Simon?
Simon I'm thinking.
Colin (*mocking*) Thinking!
Lucy Leave him alone.
Colin Thinking about what? Don't you like the zoo?
Simon Yeah. I like it all right.
Colin You could have fooled me.
Melanie Come on Colin. Let's go.
Colin Right . . . you two can come if you want. We're going.

Melanie and Colin leave.

Lucy Do you want to go with them?
Simon No.
Lucy What about seeing the sea-lions?

Simon   Not bothered.
Lucy   We can't though. They've got the guide book and we don't know when feeding time is . . .
Simon   Ask somebody.
Lucy   I will if you want to see them as well.
Simon   There's only one thing I want to see.
Lucy   Oh?
Simon   You wont like them.
Lucy   Why not?
Simon   You wont.
Lucy   Well tell me.
Simon   Snakes.
Lucy   Snakes!
Simon   I told you.
Lucy   They're slimy and poisonous.
Simon   Not all of them. I'm going to see the snakes. Come with me Lucy.
Lucy   No thanks.
Simon   I'll give you an orange if you do.
Lucy   I don't want an orange.
Simon   A packet of crisps?
Lucy   And an orange?
Simon   OK.
Lucy   All right then. Where are they?
Simon   Over in the reptile house.

They walk off quickly to find the snakes.
There is a quiet in the reptile house. All sorts of snakes are there. They slide around noiselessly.
Simon *and* **Lucy** *stand watching a large snake spit his tongue out and back.*

Simon   Look at that Lucy.
Lucy   That could kill you.
Simon   Some snakes can swallow people.
Lucy   Can they?
Simon   I wouldn't mind having a snake.
Lucy   It might swallow you.
Simon   Not if you fed it.
Lucy   What do they eat?
Simon   Mice, birds, rats, frogs . . . anything like that.

The **Teacher** *arrives.*

Teacher   Hello you two. Enjoying yourselves?

Lucy Yes thanks.
Teacher What have you found?
Lucy Snakes.
Teacher What sort of snakes?
Simon Rattlesnakes.
Teacher They look deadly.
Lucy Are all snakes poisonous?
Simon No. I told you once.
Teacher Most are though aren't they Simon? It's hard to know which aren't unless you're an expert. I wouldn't like to find out the hard way.
Simon Some squeeze you to death. Some poison you. Ask the keeper.
Teacher That's a good idea Lucy.
Lucy All right.

The **Teacher** *and* **Lucy** *walk away to find the keeper.*

Lucy Hello.
Keeper Hello.
Lucy Can you tell us something about snakes?
Keeper Something about snakes! Well there's so much about snakes to know. Anything in particular?
Teacher We were talking about which ones were poisonous.
Keeper Most of the ones here are poisonous. Look. (*He points to a snake*) Can you see how his eyes stare?
Lucy Yes.
Keeper He can't blink you see. He's got no eyelids. He has a layer of clear skin . . . like windows.
Lucy Oh yes.
Teacher That's why they look so frightening . . . staring like that.
Keeper And this big one here — this python. He attacks deers and tigers and then swallows them — whole!
Lucy That's what Simon said.
Teacher By the way, where is Simon? (*He looks round*) I'd better go and catch up with him and check on the others. Come to the coach in five minutes Lucy.
Lucy All right.
Keeper Snakes started as underground lizards who lost their legs because they had no need of them crawling about in their tunnels. And their eyes closed because they didn't need to be able to see — and when they came to the surface and tried

living there the skin slowly cleared and became transparent. Snakes are very interesting.
Lucy   It gets creepy in here when you talk like that.
Keeper   They're harmless enough where they are. As long as they're in their tanks and cages they're all right.

Later in the afternoon the children are settled on the coach ready for the journey back to school.

Teacher   Everybody here? (*He counts*) Twenty four. That's right. OK driver.

They set off. **Simon, Lucy, Melanie** *and* **Colin** *are sitting together.*

Melanie   You should have seen the tigers. They were dead hungry — they were roaring at everybody. Then the keeper came and chucked them great big lumps of meat.
Colin   Horses heads . . .
Lucy   Horses heads?
Colin   They were you could tell.
Lucy   Rubbish.
Melanie   What did you do anyway?
Lucy   Went to the reptile house.
Melanie   Boring.
Lucy   Snakes aren't boring. They can kill.
Colin   Was that your idea Simon?
Simon   (*not taking much notice*) Yeah.
Colin   You never speak Simon. What's up with you?
Simon   I'm thinking.
Colin   What about? You were thinking last time I asked.
Simon   I was thinking then about how I could get a snake . . . I'm thinking about what I can do with it now that I've got it . . .

* Which animal would you be most interested in?
* What is Simon thinking at the end of the play? Do you think he regrets taking the snake?
* It was wrong to take the snake.
  Why did Simon do it and do you think he knows enough about snakes to have chosen one that isn't dangerous?
* Have you ever had the urge to steal something?
  What sort of feeling is it?

* Find out as much as you can about one zoo animal and write some notes on it to include in a zoo guide. Put the work of the class together and produce a guide book for an imaginary zoo.
* Write a poem called *'Snake'*.
* Mime the movements of as many animals as you can. Which ones are you best at? Try to work out a movement and mime called *'Animals'*.
* A man once sat in a glass cage full of deadly poisonous snakes. He was there for many days trying to break a record. He had to move very slowly and carefully and not be afraid when the snakes slithered over him.
  Imagine you are that man and write down your thoughts as you look around at the snakes and observe people watching you from outside. Television cameras are there, and press photographers.
* Work out what happens next on the coach and start where Colin says . . .
  'You never speak Simon. What's up with you?'
* Imagine Simon eventually telephones the zoo and admits he took the snake. Write the conversation Simon might have as he speaks into the telephone.

UFO

Kate	Woman
Sue	Alien 1
Graham	Alien 2
Robert	Alien 3

It is a mild autumn evening. The lights in the town are twinkling in the distance as four friends are walking home from the youth club.

Graham I'm fed up with the youth club.
Sue So am I. I'm not going again.
Kate It's better than staying in all the time.
Sue It's a waste of time.
Kate You're always moaning.
Sue I'm not. Graham thinks it's a waste of time as well.
Graham Nothing happens in this place. It's dead.

Kate *looks up into the dark sky and notices an object flying towards them.*

Kate Look at that. In the sky.
Graham What?
Kate There.
Graham I can't see anything.
Kate Just over the top of that building.
Robert Oh yeah, I can see it.
Sue Flying saucer!
Graham Rubbish.
Sue It must be.
Sue It is . . .
Robert It's coming this way   and it's getting lower.
Kate It's going to land in the school playground — come on.

They run to the nearby school and climb over the gates into the playground.

They hide behind the cycle shed and watch. The object lands quietly and a door opens. Three aliens climb out.

Alien 1   (*jumping up and down*) The ground here is solid.
Alien 2   Yes it is. Not what we expected.
Alien 3   And there is a building. It is a strange shape.
Alien 1   Yes. It is a box. Notice the corners. They are dangerous.
Alien 2   We must take a sample of the ground.

He bends and starts chipping at some of the playground.

Alien 3   This could serve us very well as a base.
Alien 1   There is obviously life Number Three. Who else could have put up the buildings?
Alien 3   They could have grown Number One. Out of this solid earth could grow buildings; other shapes and forms. We don't know. That's why we are here. To find out.
Alien 1   Apologies Number Three.
Alien 2   (*still digging*) I have found a soft base to this material. It is a hard skin on top of a soft base.

He puts the sample in a bag.

Alien 1   Wait a minute. What is this?
(*He sees an old newspaper on the ground. He gets it . . .*)
This is a valuable find. Look. I have not seen anything like this before.
Alien 2   (*pointing to a photograph*) What are these?
Alien 1   They might be representations of life here.
Alien 3   Yes. I think I understand. That must be what the beings look like . . . (*They all laugh*)
Alien 1   (*opening a container*) We must remember to take some of this gas back with us. (*He grabs some air and puts the top back on*) We would die in this. We must find a way of existing in it if we are to return to take over.
Alien 2   It has been a good night Number One.
Alien 1   I agree.
Alien 3   Our leader will be pleased. We should return again soon.
Alien 1   Tomorrow. We will return tomorrow. When darkness protects us we will return.

A cat wanders across the playground. It goes up to the aliens and rubs against their legs.

Alien 3   What is this comrades?
Alien 2   The life of the planet!

Alien 1   I can't see how. It doesn't look very intelligent.
Alien 2   What else could it be?
Alien 3   We can't know. They look easy to dominate Number One.
Alien 1   If this is all we have to conquer then our job will be easy.
Alien 2   We could take it back with us.
Alien 3   Good idea Number Two.

Number Two *picks it up and puts it into the craft.*

Alien 1   It might die on the way or disappear altogether as we fly through the time zones. But we will take the chance. Let's go.
Alien 2   Have we a correct space bearing Number One?
Alien 1   Yes.

They climb into the craft and take off.

Graham, Robert, Sue *and* **Kate** *are speechless.*

Sue   Well?
Graham   I can't believe it.
Kate   Who said it was boring round here?
Graham   Nobody'll believe us.
Kate   They'll have to.
Graham   Why will they?
Kate   We saw it didn't we. We all saw it.
Robert   They said they were coming back tomorrow.
Kate   They did. Let's come back ourselves.
Sue   We could bring a camera.
Graham   But nobody else. This is our bit of action.
Sue   We could send a picture to the paper.
Kate   Good idea. Let's get out of here now though.
Robert   Right.

They climb over the gates and into the street.

Kate   Meet tomorrow then?
Graham   Sure thing. Everybody agree?
All   Yeah.
Graham   Right, and don't tell anybody.
All   No.
Graham   Swear . . .
Kate   Don't be soft Graham. Nobody has to swear anything.
Graham   No need to be like that Kate.

They are disturbed by a woman walking along the street making cat noises...

Woman Here puss... puss... puss... here puss... sh... shhhh... shhhh. You haven't seen a black and white cat have you?
Robert Yes...
Kate (*shutting him up*) No. We haven't.
Woman Oh?
Robert It was black, the one we saw.
Woman That's funny. He never usually stays out.

She moves on...

Kate Tomorrow night then?
Graham OK.
Robert What time?
Sue Eight o'clock?
Kate Right... eight...

The following evening the four are settled behind the cycle shed waiting...

Robert Can anybody see anything?
Sue Not yet.
Kate Give them time.
Graham Got the camera ready?
Robert Yes.
Graham Right... we just wait...
Kate Look!

Kate points to an object in the sky which appears to be moving towards them.

* Why are the young people afraid of the aliens? Do they have anything to fear from them? Would you have stayed hidden?
* What is a UFO? Have you ever seen one? Do you know anyone who has? Have you ever read stories about UFOs?
* Do you think there could be life on another planet? What do you think it could look like?
* With a friend, imagine that one of you thinks they have just seen a UFO. They are trying to convince the other one who doesn't believe them. Act out the conversation.

* Write your own poem called UFO.
* Imagine you are one of the aliens. Write a report on the way back to base on what you have observed.
* Write what happens next in the play. You can write it in play or story form and include new characters and places if you like.
* Imagine Kate, Graham, Sue and Robert take some pictures of the aliens when they return and that the pictures get on the national news. Work out a television programme where they are interviewed and asked about what they saw.
* Draw a picture of the aliens — show what they are like from front and back views and also draw a picture of their space craft. If you have time you could make a sketch of part of their planet.
* Work out and act a scene where Kate and her friends are taken to the alien's planet. Show what happens to them as they are spoken to by the leader.
It might begin . . .
Leader: So you are from the planet Earth?
Kate: Yes.
Leader: We call it Madron.
Kate: Oh . . .
Leader: You are going to help us to conquer Madron . . . and this is the way we'll do it.

Paws

Tim
Woman
Girl

Alfie
Lorraine
Policeman

Tim, **Lorraine**, *and* **Alfie** *are on an adventure club camp with their school. They are in a thickly wooded area. It is dark and getting colder.*

Tim (*shivering*) Time we went to bed.
Alfie   Yeah, it's getting colder.
Lorraine   Two more days.
Alfie   I'll be glad to get back.
Lorraine   Not me. I like it here.
Tim   Suits me as well.
Alfie   I've had enough.
Tim   Have you?
Alfie   There's more to do at home.

Pause . . .

Lorraine   Oh well – everyone's gone to bed. I suppose I'd better. See you in the morning.
Tim   'Night Lorraine.

Lorraine *begins to leave. She stops suddenly in her tracks as she hears a scream.*

Lorraine   Did you hear that?
Tim   What was it?
Alfie   It came from down in the valley.

There is another scream . . .

   There it is again.
Tim   Let's go and have a look.
Lorraine   Don't leave the camp.
Tim   Do you think we'd better wake the others?

Lorraine No.
Alfie Let's just sit and wait. It might be an animal or something. Forests are full of weird noises.

The scream is heard again.

Alfie It's getting nearer.
Tim Yeah, it is.
Lorraine It's not an animal either is it? It's a girl.
Alfie I can hear running.

They listen as the footsteps get nearer. **Tim** *calls out.*

Tim Who's there? Hello . . .

A **Girl** *staggers, breathless, towards them.*

Alfie What's up?
Girl (*breathless*) She's . . . she's . . . after me . . . she's . . .
Alfie Who is . . . what's wrong?
Lorraine Sit down.
Girl I can't . . . she's after me . . . she's coming . . .
Tim Who is?
Girl She is.
Lorraine Why is she chasing you?
Girl (*trying to run*) I've got to get away.
Lorraine (*holding her*) Wait a minute. Get in my tent.
Girl What?
Lorraine Come on. Get in my tent. We'll hide you.

Lorraine *takes her to the tent.*
Voices can now be heard coming through the trees.
Lorraine *returns.*

Tim Who is she?
Lorraine Don't know.
Tim Where's she from?
Lorraine Don't know.
Alfie You should have asked.
Lorraine She's frightened to death . . . she's shaking like a leaf.
Alfie So am I.
Tim We'll pretend we don't know anything.
Alfie OK.

A **Policeman** *and a* **Woman** *arrive. They too are breathless.*

Woman What's this?
Alfie (*nervously*) We're camping.

Woman Where is she?
Alfie Pardon?
Woman The girl.
Policeman Have you seen anyone come this way . . . a young girl?
Lorraine No.
Policeman Did you hear anything?
Lorraine A bit of a noise but we thought it was animals.
Woman (*To* **Policeman**) They're lying, they must be.
Policeman I told you I thought she went the other way.
Tim We haven't seen anybody — honest.
Woman If you do see a young girl, you be sure and let the police know.
Policeman We'll call back tomorrow — to check the camp. Where's the person in charge?
Tim He's asleep . . . has been for ages.
Policeman (*To the* **Woman**) Come on then. I think we're wasting our time in the dark.
Woman I say we carry on. She can't be far away. I'll catch her if it's the last thing I do.

She runs off followed by the **Policeman**.

Tim What do we do now?
Alfie Go and find out about her Lorraine.
Lorraine All right.

She goes to her tent and returns a second later . . .

She's asleep.
Alfie So?
Lorraine She's tired out.
Alfie So?
Lorraine I'm not waking her Alfie. We'll ask her in the morning.
Alfie We need to know now. If she's done something wrong we could be in big trouble.
Lorraine We'll have to take a chance.
Alfie Why?
Lorraine How would you like it?
Tim She's right Alfie. Let's leave it till the morning.
Alfie I won't be able to sleep.
Lorraine I'll leave her where she is. I'll go and squeeze in with Carol and Annette for the night.
Tim I wonder who she is?
Alfie I say you wake her and find out.

Lorraine (*angry*) Well we're not going to. Not till the morning. Goodnight. (*She leaves*)
Alfie You never know who she might be . . .
Tim Come on. We'll know about her soon enough.

They go to their tents and sleep.

Lorraine *wakes early and goes to check on the* **Girl**. *She is amazed by what she finds. She runs to wake* **Tim** *and* **Alfie**.

Lorraine (*outside their tent*) Tim . . . Alfie . . . wake up.
Alfie What's wrong?
Lorraine Come out.
Alfie Why?
Lorraine Come out.
Tim (*waking*) What's going on?
Lorraine Quick you two.
Tim What's the matter?
Lorraine The girl's gone.
Alfie Good.
Lorraine That's not all . . .
Tim (*getting up and out of the tent*) What?
Lorraine The tent's been flattened — and it's covered in paw marks . . .

* Who do you think the girl is and why is she running away?
* Were they wrong to lie to the woman and the policeman? What would you have done?
* Where is the girl the next morning, and what are the paw marks?
* Have you ever been camping? Did you have any strange or unexpected things happen to you? If not, were you at any time a little afraid of or worried by the dark or the strange sounds around?
  Write an account of your strangest experience.
* With a friend work out the conversation Tim and Alfie could have had before they went to sleep.
* Make a list of words to describe how everyone in the play is feeling.
  Share your words and ideas with the class.
* Write these words on pieces of paper and put them in a box. Take them out one by one and try, in turn, to mime or imitate the emotion or meaning of the word.

One of the words might be the start of an idea for a new story of your own to perform or write.
* Work out and perform a mime story which shows a person or animal being hunted by others.
* Continue the play either by acting or writing the events which follow. You could start with the three young people following the paw prints into the woods.
* Write your own story, play or poem called *Claws*.

The Word

Bosie
John
Richard

Slim
Jim
Neil

Bosie *is the leader of a gang in school. He likes to push other people around, and decides to pick on* **Jim**.

Bosie (*approaching* **Jim** *in the cloakroom*) All right Jim?
Jim Not too bad.
Bosie Know what the word is Jim?
Jim (*puzzled*) What?
Bosie Know what the word is about you?
Jim No.
Bosie Word is you're 'yella'.
Jim Oh yeah?
Bosie Yeah. (*Turning to his gang*) That right? (*There is no response*) Well it is right whether they think so or not. Slim says you're 'yella'.
Jim Who's Slim?
Bosie You know Slim.
Jim No I don't.
Bosie He knows you — says you're 'yella'.
Jim Does he?
Bosie Are you?
Jim Am I what?
Bosie 'Yella'.
Jim Don't know.
Bosie Don't know! Course you know; everybody knows whether they're 'yella' or not. I'm not 'yella', (*Looking at his gang*) These boys aren't 'yella'. They know they're not 'yella'.
Jim I might be — I might not.
Bosie You'd better decide because I think Slim's going to

come and see if you are. He thinks he might poke you around a bit — just to see.
Jim   (*walking away with his coat*) We'll see about that.

Bosie *turns angrily to speak to his gang.*

Bosie   What's up with you lot? Why didn't you join in?

Silence . . . .

Well come on, tell us. You'd better do better than this tomorrow. And you, Slim, you could have said something. You'd better get good at it if you want to stay in my gang.

He stamps off.

John   I didn't like that.
Richard   What did he do that for?
Slim   I never said he was 'yella'. I never said anything about Jim. Jim's all right.
John   Yeah. He's all right. I wish he'd given Bosie a clout.
Slim   I don't want to pick on Jim.
John   You know what'll happen if we don't do what Bosie wants us to do . . .
Richard   I'm fed up with him. I think I'll leave this gang.
Slim   There's no chance is there. He'll murder us. We're only in his gang because he threatens to beat us up if we leave.
John   We can all leave together . . .
Slim   Bosie wouldn't let us. I don't know what to do about Jim. I like him.

Later that evening **Bosie** *is with one of his friends at the club.*

Bosie   You should have seen Jim Banks today.
Neil   Yeah?
Bosie   Frightened him to death I did.
Neil   Yeah?
Bosie   Didn't know which way to turn. I had him eating out of my hand.
Neil   Yeah?
Bosie   If you want to see a bundle, hang about after school tomorrow. Slim's going to get Jim Banks.
Neil   Yeah?
Bosie   Slim'll have him tomorrow.
Neil   (*thinking*) Here Bosie, what's Slim getting him for?
Bosie   Don't ask soft questions.
Neil   Sorry.

Bosie He's getting him because I'm telling him to get him. I'm Bosie Reed remember?
Neil Yeah.

The rest of the gang are outside **Jim**'s *house.*

John Come on. Let's call for him.
Richard Good idea.
Slim I don't know what to say.
John We'll help you.
Richard I'll do the talking if you want.
Slim Yeah. All right.

They knock on **Jim**'s *door. He opens it.*

Jim Yeah?
Richard Fancy coming out for a bit Jim?
Jim What for?
Richard We want to have a talk with you.
Jim Bosie with you?
Richard No, but Slim is.
Jim Oh yeah? (*To* **Slim**) You the boy that's going to get me?
Slim I'm Slim.
Jim I'll get my coat.

He goes inside . . .

Richard I hope this works.

After school the next day **Bosie** *has got his gang in a corner of the playground waiting for* **Jim**. **Neil** *is with* **Bosie**.

Neil (*seeing* **Jim** *coming*) Is this him Bosie?
Bosie Here he is. All right you lot. Let's get it right today. Ready Slim?
Slim Yeah.

Jim *arrives.* **Bosie** *stops him.*

Bosie Know what the word is?
Jim No.
Bosie Same as it was yesterday. You're 'yella'.
Jim Oh yeah?
Bosie You know you said you didn't know who Slim was?
Jim Yeah.
Bosie Well he's here . . . and he says you're 'yella'. Don't you Slim? Matter of fact Slim's going to give you a good hiding now.

Jim Oh.
Bosie I'm going to watch to see if he does it right. Right then Slim . . . he's all yours.

Slim *steps up to* **Jim**. **Bosie** *steps back and stands with* **Neil**. *They form a circle round* **Jim** *and* **Slim** *who look at each other for a moment.*

Slim Jim.
Jim Slim.
Slim How's it going?
Jim Not bad. How is it with you?
Bosie (*shouting*) Get on with it Slim.
Slim You're all right Jim.
Jim So are you Slim.

They slap hands in a gesture of friendship.

Bosie What's going on?
Neil I thought you said there'd be a bundle?
Bosie (*pushing* **Slim**) Come on Slim.
Slim (*pushing him back*) Don't push me.
Jim I'll fight you Bosie.
John And me Bosie.
Richard Yeah, so will I.
Slim One at a time Bosie?
Bosie (*worried*) No, come on lads. Leave off. I don't want to fight. Come on. If Jim and Slim are mates that's OK with me.
Jim Scared Bosie?
Bosie (*moving backwards*) Me?
Jim Scared?
Bosie No.
Jim No?
Bosie (*his back is against the wall*) A bit . . .
Jim (*turning to* **Neil**) You know what the word is about your mate?
Neil No.
Jim Word is . . . he's 'yella'.

John, **Richard**, **Slim**, *and* **Jim** *walk away leaving* **Bosie** *and* **Neil** *together.*

* Have you ever met anyone like Bosie?
* Why don't his gang turn against him sooner?
* What do you think makes people into bullies? What do you think is the best way of dealing with them?
* Are you pleased when Bosie is made to look silly in the end? Are all bullies the same underneath?
* Write the part of the play where John, Richard and Slim have called for Jim and he has gone to get his coat. Begin where Richard leaves off . . .
  Richard   I hope this works.
* Write a character description of Bosie and Jim. Say what you think they are like as people. Mention their likes, dislikes, ambitions, talents, family, friends; whether they are bad tempered, kind, patient, understanding, selfish, helpful, friendly . . .
* Get some old magazines and newspapers and cut out some pictures of people to fit the character's descriptions. Stick them on to a piece of card and label them Bosie, Jim, Slim etc. . .
  Write one sentence by each picture to sum up that person.
* Write a poem called *The Bully*.
* Collect as many opinions as you can about bullies and bullying and how to deal with them. Then prepare a documentary programme which is examining the problem. You will need some facts from your own experience and some opinions.
* Try to set up a debate where the problems of violence and bullying are discussed. Start by saying what happens and how bullying shows itself, and go on to talk about what the police, schools and individual people can do to stop bullying. Remember that bullying can lead to people becoming very unhappy and desperate . . . it is a serious subject.